Walk With Me

A Journey Through Life: Hardships and Joy

By

OLUYINKA
MARCUS

OLUYOMI
MARCUS

Forward By Mark Sandford

Walk With Me

Copyright © 2018 by Oluyinka & Oluyomi Marcus

Tellwell Talent

www.tellwell.ca

ISBN

978-0-2288-0265-5 (Paperback)

978-0-2288-0266-2 (eBook)

Walk With Me

Contents

OLUYINKA & OLUYOMI MARCUS

Forward

In my thirty-three years as a prayer counselor, through inner healing I have seen many miracles and countless lives transformed. But one thing has always been in short supply—materials that infuse healing principles into our daily walk with God. *Walk With Me* is a tool that can help fill that nitch.

Yomi's poems will peak your interest, soften your heart, and prepare you to explore practical ways to walk out your healing. Then—from getting feelings off your chest, to forgiving, to establishing routines that bring structure to the chaos of life—Yinka will draw together your scattered thoughts and call you back to the simple perspective that only a loving God can provide. Once she has seated you firmly in His lap, she will give you prayers to help articulate the simple but elusive cries of your heart.

Draw close to the Lord, she says. Quiet your mind. Let Him focus your jumbled thoughts. Pour your heart out to Him in prayer. Let Him heal you. Yes, it's that simple; He wants to be there for you. If you will only stop to listen, you will hear Him calling out . . .

. . . "Walk With Me."

Mark Sandford
Spiritual Director, Elijah Rain Ministries
Co-author, *Deliverance And Inner Healing*
www.elijahrainministries.org
(Mark & Maureen head up the ministry)

Acknowledgements

First, we want to thank God Almighty for the ability and gift of writing. We are grateful to God for seeing us through the project of a mother-daughter endeavor by the power of Holy Spirit. To every person we have encountered along life's journey, we thank you. You are all very precious to us. We would like to thank our editor, Mark Sandford of Elijah House Ministries, for his mentorship input into this project. A very big thank you to Adeyinka Marcus (husband and father) and Adeyemi Marcus (son and brother) for your love and your ceaseless support. Thanks to Olusola Taiwo (brother and uncle); we are grateful for your thorough and honest proof-reading of the manuscript. Thanks, Rachel Ndembe, for helping us out at the initial stages of the manuscript. Thank you Adeola Adekugbe for your invaluable assistance, you are awesome!

Dedication

We dedicate this devotional to God Almighty, and to families experiencing hurts as they relate with one another. We pray for healing within, and freedom to live life to the fullest in joy. Walk with God! Walk with each other! Walk with us and journey through this devotional. God will see you through. Keep trusting!

Introduction

HEART SET FREE

I see people in pain
I see people writhing in pain
Why do we hurt so bad?
Why do we cause much pain?
I see people in pain! Hearts bleeding! Hearts crinkled! with wrinkles!

I see people in pain
Hearts rumpled, worn out and tattered! Fragmented!
I see people in pain
Hearts broken in pieces
I see people in pain!

Do you need the rain! Pure rain that cleanses!
Do you need the hovering? The special touch!
Possibilities are endless! Take it! Lean on! Lean in! Soak in!
I see you! I feel you! I love you!
Open up the door and I will come in! … says The Lord God of Hosts!

Yes, I need you! Oh, how I need to lean in and lean on and soak it in!
I acknowledge my pain!
Oh! how I need You Lord!
I forgive! I repent! I renounce! I lean on You! Lord! Mercy!
Teach me Your ways Oh Lord! How I need You

I surrender my pain! This troubling pain…
Fragmenting! Breaking! Tattering!
Oh, heart! I feel your pain!
Come into true rest… true peace!
Be released! Your dawn is broken!

Be free to love again! Be free to breath again! Come alive! Hope Alive!
I see you! I feel you! I love you!
Heart! Sweet Heart! Brave Heart! Loving Heart!
I call you into life! Come into My Life!
I Am! Jesus Christ! Resurrection and Life!
Take it! Freedom! Victory! Breakthrough!
New life has come!
Beautiful heart! Restored!
YOU ARE BEAUTIFUL! HEART SET FREE!

Oluyinka Marcus
Counselor/Prayer Minister
www.hopealiveministry.ca

(Special acknowledgement: John Akinde made audio recording as a spoken word piece)

Introduction

LIFE IS A GIFT!

Sometimes this is hard to believe because our experiences can be full of negativity, pain, challenges, and hardships. Many times, we want to scream, cry, or just give up. This is human. As Christians, we often think it's wrong to have negative feelings (like pain, anger, shame, and depression), so we ignore them or push them aside. We can find ourselves lost and in need of rescue. But instead of reaching out for help, we may pretend that life is perfect, even when we know it is not. We don't want others to see us struggle, so we struggle in silence and even refuse to acknowledge it to ourselves. The result is that we spend much of our time hiding and resisting, consumed in pain.

The poetry in this book was crafted to express real emotions we all have felt on this journey called life. Most of us are aware of the benefits of writing things down, expressing experiences in words, journaling, and poetry. This can help increase self-awareness and spiritual connection. This book is also a call to release pains we have kept bottled up and begin expressing them to God. This is exactly what King David did. He poured out his thoughts and feelings through the good times and the bad. His Psalms are full of words of anger, confusion, and despair. Yet, at the same, time they are filled with hope.

After reading the poems and working through the pages of this devotional, my hope is that we will recognize that your feelings and emotions are not "bad" and they should be acknowledged. I pray that we will find the courage to express ourselves in words to God. And I hope that through expressing the thoughts we hold inside, we will find peace and realize we truly can overcome the challenges of life. Psalm 55:22 says, "Cast your burdens upon the Lord." This gives us permission to express things that burden us. We can let out the pains we are struggling with. It is only through this openness that we can discover true healing and freedom. Our hope is that this devotional brings you closer to God.

Oluyomi Marcus
Author & Health Coach

Walk
With
Me

In the midst of it all

O God,
I see You daily and find comfort in Your presence;
Your word brings life to my soul.
As I turn my eyes towards You
I am filled with joy and peace;
It is You who fill my heart with rejoicing.
May my voice bring You pleasure and each word sing honour to Your Name.
May my song make Your heart melt; may the
melody of Your heart flow through me.
My desire is to bring You glory;
Each part of me longs to sing Your praise.

Addressing Past Hurts

Many factors contribute to a hurt or a broken heart. Situations or events are capable of triggering past hurts we have stored up in our minds and hearts. Storing these hurts can affect our daily lives—how we interact with others, what we think and feel about ourselves, and how we live our lives. It is our inner man that truly suffers. This is why it is so important to find out the unresolved issues of the heart and understand the hidden stories behind our irritability or unpleasant negative actions and reactions. When we are able to address our pain and hurts head on—then there can truly be a full and complete healing. Instead of merely addressing the present hurt, which could be a symptom of past unresolved hurt, we can effectively address our hurts at the source. (*Please note that seeking help from trained individuals to process unresolved emotional pain of the past is beneficial*)

The psalmist calls his soul to attention with the question, "Why so downcast?" (Psalm 42:5). Often the profound charge to "hope in God" can be lost in the trenches of the pain that result from past hurts. It can seem impossible to make the necessary change, even when we truly desire it. It can be difficult to seek help or fully address our pain when we are always feeling guilt and shame. But when we place our Hope in the Lord, the problems will not weigh us down so deeply that we become stuck for long, unable to move on well in life.

PRAYER: "Hasten, O God, to save me, Oh Lord, come quickly to help me" (Psalm 70:1).

TODAY'S BIBLE READING:
Psalm 42:1-5

Day 1 / In the midst of it all:

Have I Given Up On God?

Have I given up on God?
Have I strayed so much
That His words seem so distant
And his face so unclear?

Have I discarded every promise,
Every truth, every love,
That my mind fills with doubt
And my heart's seemingly cold?

Have I forgotten His amazing Grace,
His love without condition,
That my wrongs expand their influence
And my life is undone?

One of the most popular hymns is "Amazing Grace." It was written by John Newton, a slave trader who later became one of the most important figures in the abolition of slavery in the UK. Although he converted to Christianity after he prayed to God when his ship almost sank, he was still in the slave trade business for many years after his conversion. However, he was able to view his captives differently when he finally began to read the Bible. That's the power of the Scriptures. He experienced God's amazing grace in a unique way. John Newton set a great example.

The Bible, The Word of God, is inspired by Holy Spirit, and people are changed by reading and meditating on it. In the Bible, David says he is able to avoid sinning by storing up the word in his heart (Psalm 119:11). We get closer to God when we are consistent in studying and meditating on His word (Psalm 119:15).

We sometimes experience distance from God; our intimacy with Him slowly diminishes. "Life happens," and we lose the freedom and peace we once enjoyed. We stop making the effort to fellowship with others, especially as we get busy with pressing activities such as college and work. It is easy to continue on the path of sin when we don't feel close to God. God is so good and full of mercy that He gives us every chance to return to Him. When we read, study, and meditate on the Word of God, we are reminded of his love, promises, and grace. Let's continue to turn to Him and return to joy!

Prayer: Father God, I repent of my sin of giving up and straying from You. I return to You, Your word, Your love, and Your joy. I enter into your peace and freedom once again. Help me not to lose them again. Thank You for your forgiveness. I embrace it. In the Name of Jesus Christ my Lord and redeemer. Amen.

Today's Bible reading:
Luke 15:20-24, Psalm 103, 2 Peter 3:9

Reflections

Day 2 / Have I Given Up On God?:

I Commit Myself

Into your hands I commit my life,
Dependent,
For daily I journey through accustomed strife,
Unknowing and uncertain.

Now, slowly transformed into enhanced splendour,
Leaning not on my own understanding,
Giving You control of my endeavours;
Vindicate me and designate me whole.

Commitment is a state of dedication. It is giving our devotion and loyalty to something, a cause, or someone. Take parenting for example. Many of us get into it without giving intentional thought to the commitment required and what that means. Many of us struggle and have much to learn about our own self-care, let alone caring for another person. When we find ourselves in constant strife or feel uncertain about the next steps of the journey of life, we may find it overwhelming. What do we do? Sometimes we lash out at our loved ones, we become irritable, and our behavior becomes challenged. Let's identify the real problems causing us to become overwhelmed and address them more effectively.

The Bible shows us how strong God's commitment to humanity is. It is meant to be relational. It is consistent. It is all about LOVE. In the book of Genesis, God remained committed even after Adam and Eve sinned. God's love commitment continued to be evident throughout the Bible. He was so committed that He sent His Son Jesus Christ to teach us, instruct us, and save us. Our commitment to God is essential. It must reflect God's commitment to us. When we understand the depth of God's commitment and His purpose for humanity, we will become His reflection of true love and apply His Word to our life. God is committed to us despite our failures and the strife that seems to overwhelm us. God is eternally faithful to His Word and His love for us. We are saved by grace through faith (Ephesians 2:8).

PRAYER: Father God, teach me to love the way You love. I want my commitment to be stronger and be in line with Your commitment, Your word, and Your purpose for me. I know that You love me. Help me, Lord, to understand Your grace as I willingly surrender all to You. Let me see through Your eyes and hear Your voice with clarity so I can continually do Your will. In the Mighty Name of Jesus Christ, our Lord. Amen.

TODAY'S BIBLE READING:
Matthew 22:37-40; Galatians 2:19-22;
Romans 12:1-2; Acts 2:42

**Day 3 / I Commit Myself:

Failure... Am I?

My inner being aches,
Calling silently to the invisible.
Dreams, illusions, wishes, hopes: vanish.

My wings heavy with
Each microscopic load
As I face the prolonged wait for change,
Once again
To fail, as expected
—An almost desired end; a curse.
Pinned upon me as I lay semiconscious within myself,
Unable or unwilling to move from the tranquil night,
Motionless in a strange foul uncertain stage,
Knowingly drifting slowly away like a mad stricken maiden
Along the water's bed.

Sometimes overwhelming sadness can hit so deep that it binds us. It can hurt so deeply that the deep aches can affect every aspect of our life and cause us to feel cursed, helpless, and hopeless. These feelings can be triggered by a single event or a combination of unexpected, uncomfortable or embarrassing events or circumstances. We perceive the actions of people around us as positive or negative. Those we perceive as negative leave us spiralling down to a place of deep pain. Sometimes we feel how parents, siblings, teachers, and community leaders expect the worst of us. We hear their negative and demeaning comments. We feel their judgment and condemnation—and we take it all to heart.

Jesus Christ responded kindly and gently even when people were in sin. Ones who were condemned by society were welcomed, taught, and empowered, so that they had hope for a better future. We are to learn a lot about relationships from our Lord Jesus Christ. We can see the best in one another and learn to speak life-giving words. When hurts and pains happen, we are called to take heart, which means being courageous, knowing that we will overcome (John 16:33). We are called to be real with our feelings, acknowledge our pain to God, and allow Holy Spirit to comfort us (Psalm 23). And we are called to release forgiveness to people who cause us pain (Matthew 6:12). The last line of this poem, "drifting . . . along the water's bed," reveals the pain within. However, we can find the hope that can lead us into the river of God's great love for the healing that will restore us.

Prayer: Father God, I pray that You touch my inmost being and heal the aches and pains I am experiencing. I acknowledge that I feel overwhelmed and offended by (*name event*) _________________ by (*name person*) _________________. I ask for Your comfort. I forgive (*name person*) _________________, and I pray for Your forgiveness where I have sinned. Father God, heal my inner being and transform me into a person who experiences true deep compassion, love, and joy. In the precious Name of Jesus Christ our Lord and healer. Amen.

Today's Bible reading:

Jeremiah 29:11; Psalm 43:5; Isaiah 60:1-3; Ephesians 4:31

Reflections

Day 4 / Failure... Am I?:

Day 5

In Awe

It is You who made the sea to be;
The dark to cease,
The light to shine.
You who made the flowers bloom,
The creatures thrive,
Refreshing flow
—It is You who makes the robin sing.

You gave the eagle wings;
You, Who made this vessel live.

And of You, oh Lord,
I stand in awe.

Awe is the high respect we can feel in reverence about something or someone. It is the unique wonder that grips us by the power of Holy Spirit. As Christians, we are to allow Holy Spirit to lead us and help us perceive things differently than what our physical eyes can see. We stand in amazement at the magnificent mountains that occupy the Rockies, and the vastness of the oceans that trace our borders. There is so much beauty in this world! When we are able to fully perceive God's creation with amazement, life itself becomes an unforgettable experience.

The Bible reveals to us how we may experience God, whether by internal revelation of Who He is, or by miraculous events. Moses' first supernatural act was the turning of water to blood in the book of Exodus 7:20. One can only imagine how perplexed the people were. The amazing truth is that God, who creates such miracles, is omnipresent; that means He is everywhere. We are given the grace to sense the presence of that same awe-inspiring God here on earth. And what an amazing experience! Adam and Eve experienced God walking in the garden (Genesis 3:8); the Psalmist spoke with amazement about God's greatness and the beauty of his creation (Psalm 8). Our hope is that we will experience such awesome internal revelation and really stand in awe of God on a regular basis.

Prayer: Father God, I know within me that You are the Creator of heaven and earth. I believe. There is no doubt in me. Thank You for the grace to believe. Thank You for the experience of life and all its miracles, big and small. I repent for times when I have not acknowledged You in the achievements of my life. I know that You did all these things for me. I pray that I will continually be grateful and thankful to You for everything. Thank You, Lord, for everything, in the beautiful Name of Jesus Christ, my provider. Amen.

Today's Bible reading:
Psalm 16; Psalm 139; John. 1:14; Exodus 16:10-12

Day 5 / In Awe:

Day 6

Then He Came

Discouragement took hold of me;
Then He brings hope.
The weight of pain brought me down;
Then He fills my cup.
Darkness circled all around;
Then He brings His light.
I lay blind from whispered lies;
Then He gives me sight.
I was locked in isolation;
Then He brings comfort.
Struggle and sickness made me weak;
Then He gives me strength.
I was bound and held captive;
Then He sets me free.

Who is He who loves so unconditionally?
Who am I who receives so much?

He is . . .
"With us."

I was nothing . . . then He came to me.
I am His.

Hope in the midst of despair is the key to a turnaround in our lives. When things are not happening exactly the way we expect, hope can help us stay strong. Life can be hard. Sometimes pain can seem to last forever. We can ask God to help us look beyond the pain and start to explore the beauties and possibilities in life.

The Bible recounts stories of hope to encourage us. In the book of Esther, in a seemingly hopeless situation, God showed up and saved faithful Mordecai from his enemies. In 1 Samuel, hope arose for Hannah who was ridiculed for many years for being barren. She didn't give up; she continued to pray. God answered her fervent prayers and blessed her. Job held onto hope and stayed strong through affliction and pain. God rewarded his faithfulness. These stories give hope that God always comes through when we don't give up. Knowing that God is always with us is the most important thing. We can talk with Him, listen to Him, and hear His voice. Knowing that He is with us in good times and difficult times can help us to better address the overwhelming feeling. Jesus Christ is called "Emmanuel," which means, "God with us"!

PRAYER: Father God Almighty, I thank You for Your word. I stand with Your word that tells me how much You love me. Help me, Lord God, to always remember that You are with me, even in my darkest times. This is Your promise, and You always fulfill Your promises. Thank You, Lord Jesus, for giving Your life for me. Thank You for coming and being with me. Thank You for paying the price for the salvation of my soul. I am grateful. Father God, help me to always be grateful. In the Name of Jesus Christ my Emmanuel. Amen.

TODAY'S BIBLE READING:
Deuteronomy 31:6; Hebrews 13:5-6, 8; Psalms 27; Matthew 28:20

Day 6 / Then He Came:

Silence

I dare not speak into the unpleasant air
Or walk into the open;
I cannot.
I must not reveal my meditations
Or unlock fastened doors;
I dare not.
Alone, holding to silence like an untold treasure,
A vase in which my security lays, quiet.
Willingly, or unknowingly, it becomes my escape
—My own velvet preserved veil,
My created fortress
Surrounded by cold distant winds—blowing, hissing.
I stay,
My body leaning against invisible walls.
The truth is . . . I am terrified.
. . . Silence lends an ear.

We've all heard the statement, "silence is golden." Silence can mean that we are dealing with depression, sadness, or grief. We can find ourselves in a place of loneliness, even in the company of others. On the other hand, it is possible to enjoy a time of alone-ness for self-reflection and peace. We can identify the reason for our silence as either destructive or uplifting. The kind of silence the Bible encourages has benefits. Jesus Christ went into private places for quiet times (Luke 5:16); Moses spent time alone where God spoke to Him face to face (Exodus 33:7; 11); Elijah heard God's voice when he spent a night in a cave (1 Kings 19:9,12); David yearned for a quiet place for restoration (Psalm 23:1-3). We, as believers, are encouraged toward quietness and trust in God to give us strength (Isaiah 30:15). We can choose the quiet place that brings life and growth for the purpose of strengthening our relationship with God. We can spend time with him, focusing on Him alone, sharing our joys and pains with Him, and hearing His voice for comfort and joy.

Prayer: Father God Almighty, I release myself to You in this quiet place. I trust in Your love for me. I choose You. I acknowledge all my pain and hurts to You. I ask for the comfort of Your Holy Spirit. I ask that you heal my wounded heart and restore my soul. You are my good Father; I receive and embrace Your healing. I am made whole by You. I move forward in your strength and joy in the mighty name of Jesus Christ, my Redeemer. Amen.

Today's Bible reading:
Psalm 62; Matthew 11:28-30;
Acts 10:9-11

Reflections

Day 7 / Silence:

Day 8

Finding Forgiveness

Can I not journey without my sins,
Bitter reminders of a damned, untamed soul
Crying out for forgiveness?
Is there purity or cleansing for a murderer, an immoral
Or a lying tongue?
Who holds the same unfortunate fate
Identical to my own?

Is there life in this self-affliction?
Can my hand work to attain?
Will Godly ambition be sufficient,
Or deprivation turn the heart of a king?
Shall I throw myself at the mercy of destruction
To ensure my release,
Or turn to God Himself?

His hand of Mercy will be on me.

Guilt is one of the most crippling emotions we can face. Guilt can immobilize by damaging and destroying our emotional health. Guilt can show up when we obsess about things we did or didn't do. The wrongs or mistakes we have made have a way of holding us down. They result in negative beliefs about ourselves and about God. When we are able to learn from these mistakes, we will grow. We need to constantly meditate on the Word of God regarding how great He is at forgiving. We must ask God out loud for forgiveness and be ready to accept it.

As Christians, is it possible to journey this life without sin? Can we live a sin-free life? The Bible calls us into a life of perfection as our God is perfect, and we have been given everything we need to live godly lives. However, the Bible makes it clear that we are not completely free from sin (1 John 1:8). We know from the prayer Jesus Christ taught His disciples, that as fallen beings we will struggle with the temptation to sin, and we can ask for forgiveness from God (Luke 11:4). We must first be aware of our sin. Then we must be willing to repent and believe we are forgiven, knowing that God promises to forgive (1 John 1:9). We are blessed (happy) when we experience God's forgiveness. To help us, the Bible instructs us to "live by the spirit" (Galatians 5:16), and not hate people (1 John 2:9-11). We free ourselves and move forward when we have forgiven ourselves and others. God is greater than our hearts and our feelings. God forgives us whether or not we feel it. We are to believe and embrace His forgiveness.

Prayer: Father God Almighty, I thank You for the salvation of my soul. I thank You for Your promises. I trust in Your love for me and that You are continually purifying me. I know the devil tries to keep me in the place of guilt. I trust that You will help me to always be aware of who I am in You. I trust in Your promises. I can overcome the devil's tricks by the power of Holy Spirit, and I can stay in freedom and victory. I believe I am forgiven, and I thank You, Lord. In Jesus' Name. Amen.

Today's Bible reading:
Romans 6; 1 John 1:7; 1 John 2:1-2; 1 John 3:20-21; Isaiah 43:25

Day 8 / Finding Forgiveness:

Void (Must I journey alone?)

Is there nothing to fill my hollow being?
Empty of all source of life,
All strength slowly diminishing,
All thirst left unquenched.

Is my existence in fact purposeless?
Ineffective in its whole?
All situations now meaningless;
No longer am I in control.

Is my presence worth nothing?
Must I journey this road alone?
All hope turns to dust;
Left alone, weak, disowned.

Empty, lonely, hopeless, helpless, unfulfilled, of no reputation, unworthy, without value, worthless . . . These are just a few words we use to describe the void we sometimes feel. What causes us to find ourselves in such a state? People's words, our own words, thought patterns, beliefs, distance from God, lack of faith, and time of transition can be reasons. No matter the circumstance, the most important thing is what we do with the void.

"In the beginning, the earth was void and without form, and there was darkness." . . . Then, God spoke light into existence (Genesis 1:2-3)! And instantly there was light. According to Isaiah 55:11, we know that the word of God does not return void (unaccomplished). Therefore, when we do feel the void we know we can go to God, like David in the Psalms. In his struggle, David acknowledged the pain of his suffering and the anguish in his soul. In the midst of his distress, as if in great thirst, he would yearn for God. Psalm 42 is a great example of turning to and crying out to God. It is worth studying. We must know that we are valued by God our Creator, and that His heart breaks when we struggle. When we go to Him and ask for help, He will bring us back to hope and praise (Psalm 42:5). This is where we can receive instructions about the steps to take.

You are not alone; you do not need to journey alone. If you do find yourself in a negative state, it is important to talk to someone—a trusted friend, professional counsellor, or prayer minister who can journey with you toward victory.

Prayer: Father God, I thank You for Your love for me. I thank You that I have not been completely swallowed by experiences of anguish. I pray that whenever I feel down and the anguish within [redundant] tries to overwhelm me, help me remember that You are near, just a whisper away. Help me to be more aware of Your presence. Lead me to the place of praise even in my suffering, so I can learn from You and return to joy. In the Mighty Name of Jesus Christ, my Restorer. Amen.

Today's Bible reading:
Psalm 42; Psalm 139; Psalm 23

Reflections

Day 9 / Void (Must I journey alone?):

Routine

I awake from incomplete sleep,
My body longing, craving, unsure;
Each muscle tense, unsatisfied,
My senses drained from the inner core,
Yet my mind, pushed, demands
Forced by the thin lanes of routine,
As if in a trance I rise from another world.
Now I stand, and I watch. My robotic being
Rehearses steps like a dance of a child
—Daily, constant, rhythmic, plain,
From the moment the light enters my newborn frame.
Nevertheless, the chain continues
Like a never-ending spiral
Cast by my first conscious breath,
Draining the strong, weak, and carnal
Slowly . . .
Yet with no promise of failure.

It is interesting how routine, as good as it is, can be daunting, especially if we think that we are stuck without a choice. Routine is what we do when we follow a certain fixed sequence of actions regularly. Sometimes routines can drain us and bring up negative thoughts and feelings. The way we combat negativity is to add positivity and light to our life. We need routine for intentional commitment that helps build a sense of loyalty and purpose. It is important to identify the spiritual purpose of a routine and be focused to accomplish that purpose, for a purposeless routine would seem mundane, unproductive, and lacking in joy. Let's learn to renew our minds and change our perspectives on certain routines that are essential for our lives. This can enhance success and joy.

The Bible reveals that people need to be engaged in routines for specific purposes. The Apostle Paul had a routine of visiting churches wherever his travels took him (Acts 17:2). Jesus Christ went to the synagogue every Sabbath (Luke 4:16). Daniel was consistent in praying on his knees three times a day, giving thanks to God (Daniel 6:10). We learn from the Bible that intentionality about routines will result in fruitfulness. We must not give up; we need to achieve success in our spirit. One of the routines the Bible instructs us about is spending quality time with God in prayer and meditating on His written Word. Adding these activities to our daily routine brings life; they are ways we can keep connected with Him all day long.

Prayer: Father God Almighty, I thank You for routines in my life. Help me identify purpose and rejoice in the outcome of each of them. I want to know Your will for my life and embrace life. Thank You for abundant life through Jesus Christ my Savior. I choose joy today, as I learn to see You in all of my life circumstances and actions. I pray that Holy Spirit will help me remember to always be grateful. In Jesus' Mighty Name. Amen.

Today's Bible reading:
Ephesians 2:10; Joshua 1:8

Day 10 / Routine:

Peace

Each piece . . . every untouched fragment
I give to You;
My annual collections . . . or sorts
—Dreams, hurts, and pains
From daily life and existence
—I place them hesitantly, in expectancy
At Your feet,
A load too great.
And I wait.
. . . And You reached me with perfect PEACE.

Many have referred to peace as a day or season without problems. Peace can also be defined as harmonious times when there is no disagreement. People can have peace within, even in the midst of chaos. Peace is inner contentment—a state of inner calmness and undisturbed tranquility. We can learn how to be at peace with ourselves and others. We must face the problem, do what we need to do, and diffuse the inner turmoil.

Many things cause chaos in our lives. These include worry, stress, shame, guilt, denial, hurt, not identifying problems, not seeking help, disappointments, certain circumstances, and struggles. Where is our place of personal harmony (peace) when we feel overwhelmed with the roller-coaster of life? Lets ask ourselves what "peace" means to us. Is it about being positive? Happy? Contented?

Peace is a gift from God. Peace, in Hebrew, is *shalom,* which means well-being, inside and all around us. Before His death on the cross, Jesus Christ comforted His disciples with the gift of His peace, and He distinguished it from the peace we get from our world. He encouraged them not to let their hearts be troubled or afraid (John 14:27). Later on, Jesus Christ reminded them that their peace was found in Him, and that they were to be glad because He has overcome (John 16:33). We can be comforted by these words, knowing that Jesus Christ gives us His peace as we give our lives to Him and trust Him.

Prayer: Dear Father God, I thank You for the peace that comes from You alone. I thank You that You have given me peace that surpasses human understanding. I give You all my worries and stress. I receive Your peace. I ask that You help me in life's challenges. I rest in the assurance that I will find rest for my soul whenever I need it. Thank You Lord. In Jesus' Holy Name. Amen.

Today's Bible reading:
1 Peter 5:10-11; Philippians 4:7; Colossians 3:15

Reflections

Day 11 / Peace:

So Far Away

My anguish cries, diminished into softened whispers.
Into the darkness my voice sits, floats
As if expecting an answer; desiring, wanting, needing—even an echo,
Or maybe growing, accepting, or slowly fainting.
Vain efforts seem to surface and place their bets
As my heart grows tired and mind confused, full,
Unable to understand, see; limited by my present view,
Or maybe falling victim to evil's heavy plan,
Taken captive by lonely hands, closed and alone!
Or maybe I've run too far . . . and lost hold.

The feeling of disappointment is common. People fail to be there for us in the ways we want them to. They are not there when we need them the most. They fall short of our expectations. Sometimes we don't feel heard, valued, and acknowledged. Sometimes we feel lonely even though we are always surrounded by family, because we don't feel understood. Sometimes we are not able to confide in people because we feel judged and undermined. We try to keep our distance, and we isolate ourselves. We may think that nobody cares and everyone seems far away. In loneliness or isolation we feel disconnected, and healthy communication becomes a challenge.

We will overcome the pain of loneliness when we seek a safe outlet where we can genuinely tell our story and address the issues surrounding it. No matter the cause of our loneliness or how deeply isolated we have felt, it is important to understand that we cannot be too far beyond hope of reconnection and joy. Jesus Christ is our greatest model. He connected with His Father when He felt lonely. In John 16:32, His connection with His Father God helped him in times of rejection. David cried out to God when he felt "desolate" (lonely) in Psalm 142:4-5.

Prayer: Dear Father God, I thank You for the life You gave me. I know that in this life I will face trials and suffering. As Jesus Christ stated, I am not alone, because my Father is always with me. Thank You, Father, that you will never leave me lonely. I come to You for comfort and wisdom on how to move forward, out from the place of loneliness. I pray that You help me reconnect with people of Your choice and with You. Thank You for Your comfort. I forgive everyone who contributed to my experience of loneliness. I thank You for healing and restoring my soul back to Your joy. In Jesus' Mighty Name. Amen.

Today's Bible reading:
Psalm 25:16; Psalm 142

Reflections

Day 12 / So Far Away:

Past

Do I call on yesterday?
Yet she comes
Like an inerasable vision . . . a nightmare
Bringing ancient pain and hurts to surface,
Once dead, at least by the shade of night.
But she . . . she returns resurrected by day,
And lurks toward the present with foul, once forgotten wind,
Undesired.
Did I call on yesterday?
Yet she's here
In a mortal memory,
Breaking me, slowly, into tomorrow's mist,
Taunting my tears, again.
Will I call on yesterday?
Will she go . . . just to come back again today?

Letting go of the past and looking forward to a better future are two important actions we must take toward full awareness of who God has intended us to be. We can accomplish both by being willing to identify the truth about the pain and allow God to help us. Pain from hurt of disappointment can sometimes be expressed as anger and fear. Our anger (and other difficult emotions we struggle with), is usually a result of an unresolved hurt from the past.

The Bible encourages us to deal with the past. Before we can let go of our past, we must process our hurt and disappointment with God. The invitation to this is for everyone. We intentionally come into His presence to address issues for the sake of fulfilling our destiny. We have overcome when we remember the hurt of our "yesterday" without being consumed by its overwhelming pain.

It is then that we will be able to find hope in God's promises. As He promised the Israelites a good future (Jeremiah 29:11), so He promises us. His promises are YES and AMEN! That means they are always true and will always come to pass. We believe and we take hold of His promises until they happen, because they will surely happen.

Prayer: Dear Lord, I confess that I have kept a lot of the pain of my hurts within me and I have not processed things with You to allow for true healing. I have allowed my "yesterday" to influence my "today," which has clouded my thoughts about Your will for my future. I repent, and I ask for healing. I forgive all those who have hurt me. I forgive myself for allowing hurts and disappointments to control my behaviour and thought processes. I move forward because I trust in You. I embrace Your forgiveness. Thank You, my Lord. In the precious Name of Jesus Christ, my Redeemer. Amen

Today's Bible reading:
Philippians 3:12-15; Isaiah 43:18-19; Psalm 51

Day 13 / Past:

Day 14

The Unlovely

I tread these desert roads alone,
Concealing all that remains of me
—Bruised and unwanted, like useless gold,
Masking all that I hold,
My heart downcast and shattered,
My spirit confused and battered.
All I believed in turns away . . .
Every dream I hold turns grey.

I stand alone in isolation
And search for an invisible God,
Pulled away from His loving arms
Where I once felt secure and calm;,
My spirit slowly growing weak.
Lord, It is You that I seek!

Sometimes we get down on ourselves. We feel we are not wanted, accepted, or regarded as worthy by people around us and those we care about. These thoughts can overwhelm our mind, heart, and body. The cause can be from past experiences of being left out, overlooked, unwelcomed, ill-favoured, unsought, rejected, excluded, or feeling unloved. Sometimes our minds create expressions that confirm demeaning attitudes, behaviours, and detrimental words spoken to us. We allow people's behaviours to affect us negatively. We allow present situations to influence what we do and determine who we are. Our spirits can be crushed by these kinds of relational issues.

We must understand that what other people do or think does not determine who we are or who we can become. What is important is how God sees us! In difficult situations, God wants to lift us up and promote us. We must forgive those who caused us to feel rejection and ask God for restoration.

In Jeremiah 29:10-14 we see that the people of Israel were in exile, captured and battered. They had been forced to live in foreign lands for so long that their dream of a peaceful life was shattered. They were ill-treated, feeling unloved, hopeless, and helpless. Despite their condition, prophets such as Jeremiah believed the promise of God and wrote encouraging words to them. God promised to prosper them and give them hope and a future. And He did.

PRAYER: Dear Father God Almighty, I come to You for comfort. Heal me, oh Lord, where I have been bruised by people's rejection. I pray for a special touch from You. Let me sense Your presence. Father God, You are my comfort and my restorer. In times of difficulties, help me know how much I need You. I trust that You will cleanse me and make me whole again. In the marvelous Name of Jesus Christ, my Redeemer. Amen.

TODAY'S BIBLE READING:
Jeremiah 29:11-14

Reflections

Day 14 / The Unlovely:

The Breath of Life

When He spoke the words, they came to be
Subject to His voice, as servants to a king.
The light flashed into a radiant glow
As rivers, from nothing, begin to flow.
Plants took root, emerging from virgin lands.
The stars glazed the heavens with one touch of His hand.
The moon appeared, fixed as lantern of the night.
The sun danced; a candle glittered bright.
Creatures gathered by air, land, and sea.
In His name all these came to be.
And at last . . .
He breathed,
And I . . . became . . . "living soul."

As children of God we are spiritual beings, and our spiritual nature is linked with that of Jesus Christ. God's intent was, and still is, to implant his divine nature of love and mercy in us. The Bible begins with the story of the creation of Adam and Eve, where God said, "Let us make man in our image and likeness" (Genesis 1:26). In Psalm 139, David writes that God knitted us together in our mother's womb. He knew us. We know, then, that we were born for a divine purpose.

It doesn't always seem like we are children of God. We make mistakes throughout life, and often make choices we know are not in line with God's destiny for us. Its important to know that we need not give up our Christianity because of our mistakes; we have a great future in God's kindness and forgiveness. God's love for us is huge! We are constantly forgiven when we sin. The most important thing we must understand about God is that He desires that every human being come to the knowledge of truth (1 Timothy 2:4).

PRAYER: Father God Almighty, I know that You created me. I am grateful for the revelation that I am created by You and I belong to You. Thank You for the blessing of my parents and my family. Thank You for the family of Christ—the Church. I pray that You help me to know Your truth about them and to celebrate them in love. Thank You for Your love within me that is helping me to live for You and to live in peace with others. Help me, Lord, to see people as You see them. In Jesus' Mighty Name. Amen.

TODAY'S BIBLE READING:
Isaiah 43:1, 5-7; Romans 8:16-17; James 1:18

Reflections

Day 15 / The Breath of Life:

Ephesians 2

The Artist studies the unshaped clay
And imagines a sculpture of greatness
One in which He can delight, and hold
Even more precious than gold.
Smiling, He begins His work, each touch carefully ordered;
He crafts each curve, each crevice with gentle tender hands.
Silence . . .
All but the song of His beating heart.
Finally, finished, He steps back to behold.
"Beautiful," He whispers . . . "Wonderful as gold."
The Artist turns to see the ground filled with piles of clay.
For each, the same vision, He began His work,
Each magnificently sculpted . . . all wonderfully made.
The Artist, in His greatness, places into each . . . a piece of Himself.
Then He smiles . . . and calls them . . . great.

 Oluyinka & Oluyomi Marcus

It is great to know that by the grace of God we have been saved by Christ Jesus. It is by revelation that we know that God created us with specific purpose and destiny. God stated after creating everything, "This is 'good.'" Each one of us was made in His likeness, and we are "wonderfully" made. Ephesians 2 explains it beautifully. As Christians, we can find joy and comfort in life's mishaps. This is also powerful, because by the grace of God we become more aware of sin and we can seek God's ready available forgiveness; "He is rich in mercy" (Ephesians 2:4).

It is the grace of God that helps us become more aware of Holy Spirit. This is a gift from God for those who believe. Whatever challenges we face in life need to be viewed in light of our salvation. That is, after we have talked to God about our pain, we release it all to Him and return to joy. The most important aspect of this process is to make sure we bring our problems to God quickly, so that we can return to joy faster and continue to be who we are called to be.

Prayer: Dear Father God Almighty, Creator of heaven and earth, I thank You for giving me revelation of who You are through Your son, Jesus Christ. Thank You for my salvation. Thank You, Lord, for Your grace. I believe that I am saved by grace and am forgiven all my sins. Help me, Lord, to become more aware of Holy Spirit and to ask You for forgiveness. Help me, Lord, to be more aware of Holy Spirit so I will not continue to fall into temptations. I live for You, my Lord. Thank You for your grace that sustains me. In the Mighty Name of Jesus Christ, my Savior. Amen.

Today's Bible reading:
Ephesians 2

Day 16 / Ephesians 2:

You Fill My Heart

You fill my heart with the sweetest song,
And capture it like the gentle laughter of a child.
Your touch, too amazing, envelopes me;
I am lost for words,
Undone.
Empty of all but You,
Your very essence is all I need.
You lift my spirits;
A prisoner . . . now free
And . . . Oh! . . . Your Love,
Your perfect love . . .

Take a minute and look inside your heart. Of course, each of us has one. It sustains life by pumping blood through the body. But the inner self is also known as the "heart" (1 Peter 3:3-4), and it is just as powerful and intricate as the biological heart. The inner self is the place where we feel and experience our emotions. Our emotions have the power to destroy or uplift us. They can cause changes in our physical heart. For example, when we feel love, fear, or anger, our heart can "skip a beat," race faster, and heat up. For this reason, it is very important what we allow in our inner self; it can impact our physical heart and our well-being.

So, what is filling your heart right now?

The Bible reveals to us how important our hearts are. We are called to guard our hearts; whatever is stored up there will flow out and be evident in our actions (Proverbs 4:23). In other words, our lives reflect what is in our hearts (Proverbs 27:19). To guard our hearts, we must be proactive and clear our inner self of negativity that can begin to build up there. If we are hurt by someone, for example, we must not keep it inside to grow and effect our life. Instead, we are to quickly work through the pain of it—acknowledge the pain, ask for the comfort of Holy Spirit, forgive, and repent of any part we might have contributed to the offence (if any).

Ask God to cleanse your inner self, and then learn to let it go. Fill your heart with the sweetness of the Word as well as happy and positive thoughts. That is, "cleanse the inner self." Make this a practice and a regular part of your lifestyle.

Prayer: Dear Father God Almighty, I acknowledge that I have filled my heart with resentments and bitterness when I was hurt. I pray for the comfort of Holy Spirit. I forgive those through whom the hurts came. I ask for complete healing of my heart. Help me Lord to guard my heart and make my heart pure. In the Mighty Name of my Lord Jesus Christ. Amen

Today's Bible reading:
Deuteronomy 11:18; Proverbs 3:3-4; Psalm 119:11

Day 17 / You Fill My Heart:

Internal Disharmony?

They wage warfare . . . my soul . . . and spirit.
From two worlds they come opposed,
Carnal desires—craving, thirsty.
Invisible man struggling to stand
—Both able, both strong,
One wanting to fill instant want,
The other, with divine eyes, surrendered only to Him;
Both pleading . . . calling . . . alert.

Every so often we do the wrong; we do things we don't want to do or know we shouldn't. Regretfully, we tell ourselves it won't happen again. Then, it does! And we ask ourselves why. There are many factors at work here. The reason we continue to do things we know we shouldn't can be summed up in one or a combination of the following factors: the degenerate mind of the flesh, the untrained mind/attitude, and unresolved bitter roots from the past. Bitter roots spring from judgments we make on our first caregivers, such as parents and teachers. What happens is we end up doing exactly what we judged them for doing. We can even make judgments against ourselves.

The Bible reveals the intricate fight between our flesh and our spirit. God created our flesh—that is, our physical body—as something that is good. But the word, "flesh," is also used to describe something God did not create: our carnal inclinations. That kind of "flesh" is always leaning toward doing wrong, due to its self-centeredness, ego, and carnal nature. Our spirit, on the other hand, when redeemed, is empowered by God do good; He centers it on peace and care for others. Galatians 5:17 helps us understand the war within. This verse refers to our free will to make decisions that either satisfy negative carnal desires or positive spiritual convictions. This struggle will continue as long as we are in this world. The prayer is that we will lean more toward good and choose those things that bring us closer to God and His destiny for our life.

Prayer: Father God, I surrender my internal life to You. Help me lean toward the Spirit in my everyday life decision-making. I ask for Your help. I trust in Your empowerment. I desire to always overcome my sinful ways. I desire to quickly address my hurts with You. Thank you, Lord, for helping me to fulfill these desires. I surrender. In Jesus' Mighty Name I pray. Amen.

Today's Bible reading:
Galatians 5:16-17; Colossians 3:5; 1 Peter 2:11

Day 18 / Internal Disharmony?:

Over Time

Over time, friends fail.
Strong bonds grow, to break
Slowly, the light turns to trial
And darkness gathers—a flood to make.

As time passes, dreams come and go;
New things found, old things pass away.
Daily, I cover my light from glow;
Fear anchors my feet to bay.

With time, new life begins,
Destined for death; share tears of pain.
Yet, over time, one thing remains:
The love and presence of the Father.
He is forever the same . . .

Friendships are important relationships. When we call someone a "friend," that means we care about them and like spending time with them. There are different levels of friendships. They are: 1) our 'occasionals'—people we contact occasionally. 2) Our casuals—the friends with whom we share interests and goals. 3) Our close friends—friends with whom we share specific ambitions and life goals, and who contribute to our life. 4) Our circle—friends to whom we are committed (and visa-versa) and whom we are committed to be open with, to quickly address conflicts, and to forgive each other to strengthen the relationship. This level of friendship is an investment—it is rare; so, when you find it, be sure to nurture it! It is always important to discern the level of your friendships.

Our God is relational. He models that for us through the Trinity: Father, Son, and Holy Spirit. He wants us to enjoy, and be blessed in, all our relationships. Friendships are important to Him. The Bible helps us discern good friendships, so that we do not become corrupted (1 Corinthians 15:33). The book of Proverbs tells us that in friendship, one is committed to the other (27:17). A friend loves at all times (22:24-25). Some friends stick closer than a brother (18:24). A friend gives good counsel (27:9). Our friendship with Jesus Christ, our Lord, needs to be stronger than any other. He already calls us friends (John 15:12-15).

Prayer: Dear Father God Almighty, I thank You that your love for me never changes, and that you are forever the same. I pray that I will be able to discern my friendship levels. I forgive friends who have hurt me, and I repent for hurting others. Help me, Lord, to discern and invest in the friendships you choose for me. In the precious Name of our Lord Jesus Christ, my Friend. Amen.

Today's Bible reading:
Proverbs 27:10, 17; Ecclesiastes 4:9-10; Job 16:20-21; John 15:13

Day 19 / Over Time:

Your Shoes

If I were in Your shoes, would I have come?
To accept God's will to live destined for pain,
To feel every pierce . . . every strike . . . every whip . . .
To feel angered hearts and bitter tongues.

Would I have freely laid my life down For them,
Or endured and stayed silent while my blood dripped from a sword?
Would I have come, knowing they would turn away?
You came.
You did it . . . for . . . me!

We've all heard stories about acts of love, such as giving gifts, surprise birthday celebrations, donations to charity, donating an organ to someone in need, and many other great stories of love and sacrifice. We've heard of firefighters who died trying to save people from burning buildings. When we step into their shoes, we can come to understand a little about why people do great things for others.

Jesus Christ came to earth for a purpose. As difficult as His suffering was, He knew what was coming, and He was prepared. He explains His purpose in scripture, saying He was here to bear witness to the truth—John 18:37, to save the lost—Luke 19:10, and, to suffer and rise again—Luke 24:46. Like Jesus Christ, we may have suffered betrayal, abandonment, false accusations, rejection, physical attacks, or violation. For every pain we suffer in the act of helping others, Jesus Christ is able to heal us and restore us back to joy. Let's call on Him.

Prayer: Father Lord, I thank You for the life and death of Jesus Christ. Thank You that He died so I can have life. I am grateful for my life. Thank You that I can come to You. I thank You that You are with me and You will never leave me or forsake me. I pray that in all my suffering I can turn to You for comfort and joy and be enabled to give to others. In the precious Name of Jesus Christ my Saviour. Amen.

Today's Bible reading:
1 Peter 3:18; John 19:28-30

Day 20 / Your Shoes:

A Broken Heart

Broken rubble. Pieces scattered, troubled.
They come. To play; pieces missing . . . trampled!
A jumbled heap of hurt and tears.
Memories easily pushed away,
To rebuild . . . impossible?
I call on the Maker;
He makes my broken . . . whole.

The words, "broken heart," describe the experience of intense emotional pain. Feelings can become so intense that they cause physical pain. They can even begin to cause damage to the physical heart. Sometimes the way we discipline, scold, and talk to children can cause them hurt and pain, even though we mean well. These interactions between adult and child can cause negative effects and tempt him toward negative conclusions, thoughts, and bitterness.

The Bible teaches that even though discipline can be painful, it trains us for life (Hebrews 12:11). We are also warned that discipline done in fear and anger can cause deeper pain that only God can heal (Psalm 147:3). For this reason, parents and all adult caregivers are to be diligent in discipline (Proverbs 13:24) and never provoke children (Ephesians 6:4; Colossians 3:21). Children must be taught and encouraged to call out to God when they feel hurt. Parents also need to be willing to talk with their children about their feelings and learn to discuss discipline with them. The hope in good parental discipline is that children will accept correction and learn to become fully functioning adults. Let us always acknowledge the pain of our hurts and release them to God.

Prayer: Dear Father, I ask for Your comfort and healing for my wounded heart. I trust that I can be set free by the power of Your Holy Spirit. I forgive people who humiliated me through their actions, corrections, and harsh discipline. I pray Your blessing over them. Thank You, Lord, for your love for us. In the Mighty Name of Jesus Christ our Redeemer. Amen

Today's Bible reading:
Hebrews 12:5-11; 2 Timothy 3:16-18; Isaiah 61:1

Reflections

**Day 21 / A Broken Heart:

Something More

I move on the pursuit to find
Something—anything—to fill this space,
Be it money, love, happiness, or fame;
I pause only to quicken my pace.

Seeking some things tangible and true,
Grasping far into the night cold;
Yet despite the promise of satisfaction, nothing left to hold.

We've heard that life actually gets more fulfilling when we seek for more of something tangible, especially when we are seeking to become better versions of ourselves. However, we must assess our continued search for things that don't serve us well or fill the void within. To what extent are we pursuing things like fame, career, money, love, and happiness, and at whose expense? Are we trying to address an unmet childhood need or a hidden adult desire? It is important to ask ourselves these questions to avoid overwhelming cycles of unfulfillment. Seeking is about the desire to find favourable things that will help us grow.

As Christians, we are called to seek the Lord and His Kingdom (Matthew 6:33). This should always be our first and leading pursuit. Every day we yearn for God and desire more of Him. We ask for His will to be done in our lives and ask Him to guide us. We acknowledge Him in every achievement, knowing that we would not have anything He did not give to us. Our level of anxiety and worry will be reduced as we persevere in keeping close to God and His purposes (Philippians 4:6). We will learn to trust in His promises (2 Corinthians 1:20).

Prayer: Dear Father God, I thank You for loving me despite my disobedience and distrust. I pray that I will always remember to come to You for help in every area of my life. I pray for genuine helpers who will help me succeed in life. I surrender everything to You, Lord. I ask that You lead me in every pursuit on my life's journey. In the Mighty Name of Jesus Christ my Lord. Amen.

Today's Bible reading:
Philippians 4:4-7; 2 Timothy 3:16-17

Day 22 / Something More:

Remember

I remember when my life was dark;
No one around to see me through,
And in my quiet place of shame
I secretly cried out to You.
I remember when my world turned upside-down;
My heart filled with hurt,
And in my quiet place of pain

I secretly cried out to You.
I remember when I couldn't see;
Around me, wind blew with rage,
And in my quiet place of fear

I quietly cried out to You.
I remember when I couldn't stand.
Sin became master; guilt chocked,
And in my quiet place of torment

I secretly cried out to You.
I remember when I couldn't go on alone.
Consciously I turned to you,
And in Your quiet place of Love
I willingly gave my all to You.

 Oluyinka & Oluyomi Marcus

Many of us are hit hard in life, and it feels like we are walking around in the dark. Some of us stumble so hard in the daylight that we hide ourselves away because of fear, guilt, and hurt. It is human to experience challenges and hardships in life. Though some of us experience more hardships than others, we all experience it differently—and that's just the way life is. When we are in a hardship, circumstance, or difficult time in life, it is hard to see the light or any type of freedom, joy, or solution. It doesn't take long to realize that it's a lot harder to see in the dark. The real problem begins, not when trouble comes, but when we start to align our emotions with the hardship. We begin to isolate ourselves and allow our mind and thoughts to stay in that dark place.

As God's children, we know that the only real light and solution to our problems come from the Father of Lights. Through the Epistle of James (1:17), we come to understand that God is the creator of all light, and that every good gift comes from Him. Therefore, when we find ourselves in any kind of dark place, we are to ask Him for special revelation, and allow His light back into our hearts and lives. We don't need to force it or pretend we are okay by putting up a happy front full of smiles, dancing, and fake laughter. God sees our heart. All we need to do is go humbly to God and confess our pain to Him. He desires to release His comfort and divine revelation to us in our times of need. We need to believe that God is our light (Psalm 27:1). He comforts us in our journey through the valley (Psalm 23:4) because His steadfast love will never cease (Lamentations 3:22-23), and we will come through with joy.

Prayer: Dear Father God, I am very grateful for Your Word. The Trust it inspires sets me free. Help me, Lord, to know Your Word. I know that I will find grace to help in my times of need. I look to You, oh Lord, for true direction. I ask for a fresh infilling of your joy daily. I thank You for being my help and my strength. In the great Name of Jesus Christ my Lord. Amen.

Today's Bible reading:
Hebrews 4:12-16; Psalm 46:1; Proverbs 3:5-6

Day 23 / Remember:

Heaven

When I get there,
What a wonder!
A place too great to imagine.
Joy, laughter, and song.
Sweet aroma fills the air.
I'll dance the streets of gold
And worship at His throne.
From Him light flows
—Dancing, incredible, great;
Better than any other place;
Heaven.

A question that comes up during evangelism is: "Will you go to heaven when you die?" Answers often include; "I don't know," "I don't care," "No such thing," "It's only an illusion," and "Yes; I go to church." One thing remains clear: many people do not believe in God as God-Father, Son, and Holy Spirit. They do not believe in Heaven and eternal life, and have not accepted Jesus Christ as their Lord and Saviour. If they knew and allowed the True God Almighty to reveal His Son, Jesus Christ, they would have revelled with excitement.

The revelation from God regarding the new Heaven and the new Earth (Revelation 21) is comforting to the Christian. The description of the Holy City is vividly emphasized. Nothing like it can ever be imagined. The glory of God brightens up the city—dazzling and crystal clear, walls built of jasper stone, foundations of precious stones, and streets that are made of pure gold. As believers we trust in the words of the God-revealed vision, and we anticipate the day we will set our eyes on the Holy City of God. God says, "My words are true and can be trusted" (Revelation 21:5).

PRAYER: Dear Father God, I acknowledge Your Word as truth. Help me to trust more. My home on this earth may be beautiful and comfortable, it cannot compare with the place in Heaven You have for me after my journey here on this earth. Thank You, Lord, for the grace to believe. In the Name of Jesus Christ, my Lord. Amen.

TODAY'S BIBLE READING:
John 14:1-4; Revelations 21; John 3:16

Reflections

Day 24 / Heaven:

Day

Between the beautiful dance of awakening sun
And bittersweet song of the new moon
My heart undergoes pressures, temptations, and doubt.
My feeble mind often mistakes real and imagined,
Restrained by apprehension and crippled with fear.

It often confuses right with wrong,
And I lose hold of what's true;
A cycle repeated,
Left longing for the warmth of my bed.

We often experience pressures and challenges in our day-to-day life. Life's challenges can be related to family, marriage, career, friendships, health, or life decisions. There are also pressures of success, achievement, fame, attaining a specific standard, meeting an expectation, or simply trying to "be somebody." All these pressures can trigger stress responses. They can make life unbearable and overwhelming, and lead to many symptoms such as sleepless nights, depression, headaches, and fatigue. When we experience unpleasant emotions, God wants us to come to Him. The book of Lamentations expresses all kinds of sorrows, heartaches, and pain. The key message is God's love and mercy (Lamentations 3:22-23). It is great to bring our sorrows to the Lord in the form of a lament. This is quite appropriate; when we are in distress we must learn to embrace God's love and compassion.

His faithfulness to us is great. Whenever we identify any wrongdoing, let us repent. When we experience hurt or offence, let us tell God about it and forgive the offender, trusting Holy Spirit for comfort and strength.

Prayer: Dear Father, I thank You for Your compassion and love. I am grateful that during my distress I can come to You, knowing that You hear me, and You will help me through it all. Help me, Lord, to always remember that You are there for me everyday. In Jesus' mighty Name. Amen.

Today's Bible reading:
Psalm 107:6; 1 Peter 5:7; Philippians 4:4-7

Day 25 / Day:

Take Control

Lord, take control;
Life seems out of hand.
Be the one to calm my fears,
And help me know Your peace.
Let me not be overcome by things seen,
But be focused on Your light.
Allow me not to sway far from truth,
But be even more in love with You.
For now, in the face of tribulations
When I feel lost and alone,
You see it all.
You make all things work . . . still,
Lord, take control.

Control is about having power and authority to dominate and be in charge of something. Sometimes we feel we have lost control of our lives. Other things, feelings, and people seem to dominate and influence our thoughts and behaviours. We've all heard phrases such as "Control yourself!" "Get a grip!" "Pull yourself together!" and "Take back your power." But we must understand that willpower is never enough. Never the less, whatever we value deeply requires effort and focus.

As Christians, we deeply value our relationship with God our Maker. We give Him full control of our lives. The Bible tells us clearly that we will become slaves to whatever we allow to control us (2 Peter 2:19); for example, money, lust, food, certain people, or even our own words. In Romans 5:1, we are reminded that when we put our faith in God, we strengthen our relationship with Him. We are safe and can find peace when we allow God to take control. Psalm 46:1 reveals to us that "God is our refuge and strength, an ever-present help in trouble." We can then let go of fear and accept God's strength. When God led the people of Israel, He reminded them: "Fear not. I am with you, I will be with you" (Isaiah 41:10).

Prayer: Dear Father God Almighty, I give my all to You. I repent for everything I have allowed to control my life. I surrender to You. I want You to reign in me. I give up trying to control my own life. My life is yours, and I trust in Your care. Thank You, God, in the beautiful Name of Jesus Christ my Lord. Amen.

Today's Bible reading:
Philippians 4:6-9; Isaiah 41-10-20

Day 26 / Take Control:

Day 27

Escape

I close my eyes;
All things disappear,
My mind empty,
My vision becomes so clear.
I go to a
    Different place,
A different
       Part of space
Where no one is but I . . .
      I
        Escape
          Into His arms.

Many people advise that taking a quick break or escape from hard times is beneficial. Escapes include taking a walk, reading a book, partying, watching a comedy or cartoon, dancing, and exercise. Ideally, these are good distractions; they can help keep our minds off an overwhelming problem and allow for clearer thinking. Sometimes, however, they can be used to avoid dealing with the real problem, and this can lead to isolation.

In John 15:11-32, the prodigal son chose to escape into a world of recklessness—drinking, partying, and other sordid behaviours—before he returned home. The Bible tells us that the father accepted his son back with open arms. In the same way, our Lord Jesus Christ calls us to come to Him for rest when we are weary (Matthew 11:28-30)! What a great place to escape—to God. There are many examples in the Bible of escaping to God. Moses, for example, escaped to the mountain to seek God (Exodus 19:3). And Jesus Christ went to the garden of Gethsemane to seek His Father when His soul became sorrowful (Matthew 26:36). Let us try to escape to a place of praise and worship even in our most challenging times. Let us seek His presence intentionally.

Prayer: Father God, I thank You for Your open arms. I thank You for receiving me each time I come to you. I ask for Your grace to always escape to Your loving arms. I know that nothing and nowhere can compare with Your presence. I thank You for it. In Jesus' precious Name. Amen.

Today's Bible reading:
Matthew 11:28-30; Isaiah 32:1-4, Psalm 25;20

Day 27 / Escape:

Day 28

Still

I've strayed from You;
> Still You help me.

Turned from You;
> Still You wait.

Disobeyed;
> Still You call me.

Drew away;
> Still You caught me.
> Still You sought me.
> You still love me.
> Still . . .

Throughout history, humanity has turned away from God in many ways. One way is by distorting the truth about creation. Controversies and debates have developed about evolution and the big bang theory. Recently we have been realizing that the big bang theory is collapsing, and many scientists are beginning to abandon the idea. The Bible says that God created all things, animals, and man (Genesis 1:1).

Another way humans have turned away from God is through a God-free, isolated, "I"-focused mentality. God created humanity for relationship. He desires that we are intimate with Him. The Bible reveals that sin came to the world through Adam and Eve's disobedience which caused separation from God and put a strain on their intimate relationship. Straying from God means confusion, pain, sinful acts, emptiness, and inability to fully live out our destiny. This was not God's desire.

God sent Jesus Christ to restore His will for us, and He opened the way for us to return to our Creator. Jesus Christ stated in John 6:39 that He will not lose any of the ones He has been given. As Christians, we believe that God is the Creator of the universe, and through accepting salvation we have chosen to fulfill God's desire for intimate relationship. When we find ourselves straying and begin to turn our hearts and minds from God, He is still there to redirect us and draw us back to Him.

Prayer: Dear Father God, I am thankful that You have loved me with an everlasting love. I ask that You forgive me for straying away from you in any way. I pray that You continue to draw me back to You. I want to always call on You, because Your plan for me and my future is always good. I pray that my soul will always thirst for You. I want to abide in You like a branch on a tree and bear the best fruit. I surrender to You, Lord, in the Holy Name of Jesus Christ, my deliverer. Amen.

Today's Bible reading:
Psalm 63:1-11; John 17:22-23; James 4;8

Day 28 / Still:

Day 29

If I could . . . ??

If I could know one thing
    I'd choose love.
If I could see one thing
    I'd envision God.
If I could give one thing
    I'd give joy.
My last words to the world
    Would be a song.
If I could touch one place
    I'd reach the sky.
If I could make one wish
    I'd never die.
If I could say one thing
    I'd voice truth.
And if I could live for one thing
    I'd live for You, LORD!

We have all used the word, "if," to explain something: "If only . . ." "If you had . . ." "If it was like this . . ." Using the word, "if," often means that there is a condition attached to what we are about to say. Many times we make "if" statements to cover up a mistake. For example: "If she wasn't so mean, I wouldn't have said what I said." "If you are nice to me, I'll be nice to you too." In these statements, acceptance is determined by a particular outcome.

According to Matthew 9:21, a sick woman saw Jesus and thought to herself, "If I only touch His cloak, I shall be healed." The woman took action; she touched the robe of Jesus, and she was instantly healed. Jesus Christ stated that her faith made her well. Without Him saying a word, in her heart she believed that she would be healed, and Jesus Christ knew her faith was strong.

IF ONLY we can follow our strong faith and thoughts with action. Faith is about complete unwavering trust and belief. Faith helps us in our weakness. Hebrews 11:1-6 defines faith and reveals faith actions to us. Like this sick woman, we are to always exercise our faith by the grace of God and the empowerment of Holy Spirit.

Prayer: Dear Lord God, help me to be totally depending on you for everything. Help me to trust and have faith in Your power to help me in everything, and to believe that you will send helpers my way when I need them. I desire to live for You, Lord. I desire that my ways please You, Lord. When I fail to please You, help me return to You because I trust in Your compassion and restoration. Thank You, Lord, for loving me. In Jesus' Name. Amen.

Today's Bible Reading:
Matthew 9:1-13, 18-34; Hebrews 11

Reflections

Day 29 / If I could . . . ??:

Gone Are The Days

Gone are the days I basked under broken hill
And wondered what my life would be.
Gone are the days like rainbow's end
>> To stormy rain.
Gone are the days I lead myself to unfulfilled ways . . .
And hid my light in guilt and shame.
Gone are the days like a soldier's return
>> To friendly ground.
Gone are the days oceans flowed from my pain
And my mind manufactured a bullet of brass.
>> Gone are the days.
Gone are the days; now forgotten
>> Particles in time
When I floated, uncaring and afraid.
Gone are the days.
> Gone are the days.
>> Those distant days.

When we were young, we did what children did. As adults, we put away childish behaviour and behave as adults do. Maturity—physical, mental, and emotional—is the major thing that separates children from adults. Maturity is knowing right from wrong, and choosing to do right. It is about the capability to control our reactions and to know positive ways to deal with circumstances. Gone are the childhood days where we threw temper tantrums on grocery store floors, snatched someone's toy from them because we wanted it, or screamed at the top of our lungs when we were hungry. Maturity is the ability to exercise self-control. Other true signs of maturity include refusing to blame others for our problems, and taking responsibility for our actions, being open to conversation rather than argument, stewarding our finances, practicing good self-care, and being able to listen more than talk. Maturity exudes confidence.

The most important aspect of the Christian life is the desire for spiritual growth (Hebrews 6:1). This desire and participation will lead to spiritual maturity. We long for deeper knowledge of God and to become more like Christ. The result is more consistency in studying God's word and in sensing His presence, growing in obedience, repentance, and forgiveness, practicing biblical teachings, telling people about Him, and enjoying intimacy with God. The process of spiritual growth will help us to stay humble and to understand our need for God. We rely on Holy Spirit to help us in our Christian walk.

Prayer: Father God Almighty, I am grateful for Your Word, the Holy Bible, that helps me get back on track when I am off. I thank You for Your love for me that draws me into Your Truth. I trust in Your faithfulness, that I will continue to mature by the help of Holy Spirit. I live for You Lord. Help me to be more consistent and persevere to the end. In the Holy Name of Jesus Christ my Lord. Amen.

Today's Bible reading:
Philippians 3:12-14; Galatians 5:13-26; Hebrews 5:11-14

Day 30 / Gone Are The Days:

Identified

Lost, without home, I wait.
Searching, longing,
I stand naked and undeserving,
A stranger to myself,
Tossed into a battle within;
Flesh against spirit, heart against mind,
Drained and made weak by voices of man.
While the pounding of life tears me down
I stare deep into my reflection,
At who I think I am.
My heart searches still . . .
For something; something true.
Then He came; He lifted me
And identified me
      As His own.

Do you know who you are? The search for identity Is said to begin in adolescence. It is very common to see adults in their thirties, forties, fifties and even sixties unsure of who they are, their unique personalities, or identifying characteristics. Identity issues can arise from denying, concealing, or even loathing characteristics that make us who we are. Sometimes, for different reasons, we lose a sense of our own identity, and we try to fill this empty space with many things. We soon realize that those things actually do not help.

As children of God, our identity is in His love for us, and our behaviour must reflect this truth. Our identity in Christ began at creation when God made us in His image and likeness. Jesus Christ came to earth to restore us, redeem us (Isaiah 43:1), and make us God's children (John 1:12). In Romans 14:8, we are reminded that whether we live or die, we belong to the Lord. The Bible is full of great images of who God says we are and how much He loves us just the way we are! We can be excited on our path toward fulfilling His purpose for our lives.

PRAYER: Dear Father, I am grateful that You are my heavenly Father. Abba Father. You are closer to me than I think. You have said in Your Word many times that You know me and You love me. Father God, help me walk as the amazing person you created and called me to be. You are the Almighty God, my Creator Who knows how my destiny will be fulfilled. I surrender my all to You. I am Yours, Lord. I thank You, Father. In the Mighty Name of Jesus Christ, my Lord. Amen.

TODAY'S BIBLE READING:
Genesis 1:27; Isaiah 43:1-2; Psalm 100:3

Reflections

Day 31 / Identified:

Passes All Understanding

I lie prostrate on dampened ground,
My face down, my arms stretched.
All around me raging storms grow fierce;
Winds swirl; violent, untamed howls pierce
As the rains pound heavily on my tender frame.
I lie stagnant.
Oceans fight through the savage air and crash with power and might,
And I become its boulder, its broken shore
Still unmoved.
Alone: no refuge, companion, or protection.
My eyes once searched
Only to find terror inside the thick, thick unwelcoming night.
I lie lost in hell itself.

Yet, from within me flows a silent stream,
Inside of me a quiet delight
Where in my affliction I began to rise.
My mind filled with perfect peace.
Though rendered broken by life itself,
I stand . . . alive in Him.

How many of us have ever felt lost, afraid, or consumed by life? And what do we do when there is chaos all around? Let's face it; sometimes life happens! We have all experienced chaos within when we have had to make decisions that required significant changes, and we were not sure where to turn or what option was best. We can become insecure, fearful, and uncertain.

It's in those moments that we have to decide to continue on a path of sadness, anger, pain, confusion, and disillusionment—or choose peace instead. If we want to live well, we need to find a sense of peace within and all around us. We can do many things to try and feel more at peace, but we will soon discover there is no real peace without Christ. The peace that God gives us is most beneficial and lasting.

We believe in the gift of the peace of God. His gift is not as the world gives (John 14:27). We have the hope of glory because Jesus Christ is in us (Colossians 1:2). Knowing and believing in the omnipresence of God and the truth about eternity, we know that God is not limited by time and space. He is the beginning and the end, and He was and is and is to come (Revelation 1:8; 21:6; 22:13). As mysterious as this may sound, it is very exciting. God is everywhere! From wherever we are, in any circumstance in which we find ourselves, we can allow Holy Spirit to help us tune into amazing joy and peace. He is with us and in us, and nothing is hidden from Him (Hebrews 4:13). When we surrender to God's presence, we can be more and more be at peace in Him. And that is what God desires for us.

Prayer: Dear Father God Almighty, I pray that whenever I am in the midst of chaos within or around me, when I feel alone in my struggles in life and I feel disappointed in people, help me find the peace of Your omnipresence. Holy Spirit, I ask that You shed light into the darkness for me to catch a glimpse of the greatness of God my Father. Dear Lord, I surrender to Your will for my life. I will seek You for direction, and I will patiently wait on You. I trust in You for my breakthrough at the right time. Help me, Lord, to trust You more. And may Your peace always be with me. In the great Name of Jesus Christ, Redeemer and my Prince of Peace. Amen.

Today's Bible reading:

Romans 6; Ephesians 2; 2 Thessalonians 3:16

Extra / Passes All Understanding:

Final Note

How To Write in *Walk With Me*, and Beyond

Journaling your Reflections: There is no "wrong" way to write. The only "right" way is to be open and honest with yourself. Simply allow yourself to be vulnerable. Reach into your feelings and begin to write.

1. Read the devotional of the day.
2. Spend a moment reflecting on them and see how they relate to you.
3. Take some deep breaths and allow yourself to think deeper.
4. Begin to write. You may find yourself doing any of the following:
5. Decide on a specific aspect of your life to uncover or, reflect on your life in general.
6. Express your thoughts and feelings freely in writing.
7. Write an open letter to God or to yourself.
8. Create a poem that expresses your feelings.

Addressing hurts

This book reveals real emotional pain and struggles. Our hope is that readers will, in every unfavourable emotional experience, encounter "God of all comfort" (2 Corinthians 1:3-5). Below is a suggested process of how to appropriately address hurts caused by others:

1. Acknowledge the pain to God (intentionally sharing it with God enhances intimacy).
2. Ask Holy Spirit for comfort and healing (take time to soak in His comfort).
3. Forgive (we are strengthened to forgive from a place of comfort).
4. Repent (ask Holy Spirit to reveal your own contribution to the problem).
5. Ask God what to do (practice hearing God's voice). (*Seek assistance: process the problem with a trusted individual or trained prayer minister/counsellor.*)
6. Be led by Holy Spirit in your decision, and do it!

(This is not a formula. You do not have to follow the order in which it is written here. Allow Holy Spirit to lead)

Coming soon - "Healing Hearts' Hurts" Workbook.

Epilogue

Yomi and I prayed through the journey of writing this book before we sent the manuscript to our publishers. We want to share the experience with you. As we prayed, God revealed a picture of His hands giving out the book to people. The sense was that His hands are on every copy, and, as you hold the book in your hand, you have received a gift from God. We strongly sensed that God's desire to walk with us is quite strong, and we wonder why we sometimes fail to surrender to Him completely. We believe that this book is for you, whether you are seeking someone to walk with in your life's journey; you are walking with someone in their life's journey; you need the Lord to walk with you in specific areas of your life; you sense that God is seeking you for a specific assignment and He wants to walk with you to fulfill His purpose for the sake of His Kingdom, or you need to totally surrender to God for a greater experience of Him walking with you.

God says to you, "WALK WITH ME."

"Every good and perfect gift is from above,
coming down from the Father of the heavenly lights,
who does not change like shifting shadows." (James 1:17)

Book Reviews

What a great devotional. Not only did it bring me closer to God, but also helped me work through things from my past. I felt a new appreciation for how God can use me to help others as I present my best self. Also, the reflection at the end of each devotional really helped put my thoughts on paper, making it easy to go back and reflect and feel encouraged. I would highly recommend this devotional to anyone, no matter where they are in their walk with God - Adeyemi Marcus

Excellent devotional! The layout is great, and it is easy read – Adeyinka Marcus